SILENT SOUND

SILENT SOUND

44 POEMS TO HEAR YOUR SOUL

By Julia Paige Lemke

Silent Sound: 44 Poems to Hear Your Soul
Author: Julia Paige Lemke
ISBN: 979-8-9912027-0-1

Cover art: Catrin Welz-Stein
Cover design: Julia Paige Lemke

For bookings and all other inquiries: www.julia-lemke.com

For my sisters.

May you always have courage to hear your silent sound.

Contents

Author's Note

In short, this book is about courage: the courage to meet yourself (over and over again).

This collection is my lived experience of the Strength card in the tarot. These poems whisper back and forth through timelines and metaphorical lifetimes as my rigidity and resilience become an unwavering permission to express my soul.

These poems are visual, literal, and metaphorical.

I hope you pause and play in these pages, listening in on my secrets so you may hear your own.

Your sensitivities are safe here.

If this book found its way into your world, trust that there is something inside meant for you.

I hope you hear it roar.

I:

An Infusion of Grace

Demons Break Free

Before I could hear
poetry, before I could write
notes, I had to cast jokes
dense with truth:
my first words
in years.

In solitude's dusk,
out slipped wild laughter.

Backed by a chorus
of my demons, I delivered
a defining one-woman show
like it was the last
show on earth,
the only art left in time.

My audience: rapt selves
surrendering their sorry swords.

A masterpiece broke loose:
sentience in my ribs.

I didn't care
to care anymore.

My enduring fractured
my will, my heart's footing.

My pour boiled away
my substance, my hold.

Jokes pieced together years
tenderness couldn't touch.

Jokes coated me in a callousness
I needed to carve an honest life.

As laughter sparked my horizon,
I played with words hot in my throat's kiln.

I threw reminders into my walls,
my foundation, my future—
crazing cracks unthreatened
by my certain secret
destruction. In the pit of my belly,
I let dusk ignite.

Fire glazed my front door
spilling onto my floors.

Mourning would soon mask my dawns.

As dim dried, I found arrows
etched in my cheeks: proof
that all along my body knew
the way

out.

The Day My Therapist Said *Fuck* Was the First and Last Time I Cried in Therapy

That voice in your head isn't yours
and you don't have to fucking listen
to it a second longer in your beautiful life.

The tears in her eyes, the unscripted
fuck, the fact that she couldn't even lie
about buying boots secondhand—

I believed her. As she mirrored my disposition,
my break, I could see my contortionism.
I squirmed as the emotions wheel

suddenly made perfect sense.
Tiny crusaders tugged truth from my eyes.
Of course you are confused. Of course you are

and it's okay. What if I could talk
back to not-me? Find the words
to fill my skull with my own sound?

What if the cacophony goading me
to be better, kinder, unattainably good

is a liar? A liar, I never owed my life.

What if I knew all along?
Proximity to touch held truth
captive in the back of my throat.

Words flooded my tongue,
an inky deluge of perfection.
You have everyone's permission

but your own. You are there
for everyone, but honey
who is there for you?

What if for once in your life,
you have permission
to act for you?

When You Falter

Choose any unit
of time. A lifetime, a year,
a day, a minute, a second.
Find one and live.
It is everything
you have.

When You Rationalize

What if I kept searching forever
to find the wrong in me
to explain the wrong in you?
All this soul-searching
so I don't have to see
the equal and greater
possibility: there is nothing
wrong with me.

The Relentless Answer

Relentlessly you try to solve it all,
but darling, the most beautiful answers
this life has for you will do everything
to find you, time and time again.

Cease your searching
and let your soul rest.

Find peace in the power and resilience
of not allowing every beat of your heart
to beat down on you. Let it tumble
music through your orbiting ears.

Trust that the march on
is worth every uncertain breath
for the day the sun beams down on you
laughing, happy, and

free.

Dear Ease

I dream about you but I don't mean it.
I know I can't make it about you all the time.

The "journey," healing, growth—any word
that tries to contain a lived-in wisdom—
isn't a line and doesn't lead to a destination.

You're a widening, a blurred circumference
I won't feel until I find.

How do I touch a point beyond
the radius of my known?

How do I hold what can't be touched?

When You Wonder

In the body, *I wonder*
loosely translates to
Go on, earnestly. You do
not need to know everything.

Footing, Found

I want to kiss you.
I want to run away.
I want to scream.

Why now? Why
this time? You say
we are so close, yet
I see just how far
the tide has taken me.

I kept myself afloat.
I savored the saltwater,
swam under the waves,
bloated my strength, but
I was left alone far too long.

My soul is involved now.

You want to be the one
to save me, to pucker my days
with kindness. As if acts of service
could relock my buoyant knees. As if love
was ever your present tense.
Maybe this time last year,
even last week, the tides

would have turned.

But honey, now I see
land and oh,
how much I want
to feel my feet

on solid ground.

Cartographer

Ease is letting go
of *right* for grays and colors.

Ease is knowing
right is an eraser, not a palette.

Ease is remembering
a line can only be a circle if it bends.

Silent Sound

The sun was long gone.

I could only wait so long
in the car, in our dark garage.

My workday Cinderella receded
into heavy heels and a heavier heart.

I swept myself toward our front door,
savoring the courtyard's impersonal shadows.

I noticed new grays. The moon whispered
warmth into the day's blindingly white stucco.

The palm leaves nodded and played along,
painting handprints on the walls.

In awe, I paused inside a winter I didn't remember.

As my eyes reached into endless sapphirine sky,
something like hope stirred.

Imagine my surprise when I found
wordless wishes still alive.

I swear, the sky slipped into me right then
and severed a secret into my mind.

A voice I could only name god,
stern with certain love.

My atheism, forgotten.
My fear, absent.

A voice I didn't know I knew:
crystal clear, silent sound. I didn't need my ears.

Like an announcement from the flight deck
of my soul, my life's invisible map,

a voice simply said,

This is so   much bigger   than you,

gone before my questioning
could answer.

Writing? Sharing words?
Love? Believing life?

I tried naming the secret,
but my heart is more precise.

The voice was long gone.

In its silent echo, an infusion of grace
carried me through

my yawning ceiling—winding up
a music box of stars.

II:
Instinctual Love

Grace Note

Six months into surrender, I'd stir
the golden streets with my gloom,
winding avenues shaded by the marine

layer's haze and peninsula's indigo hover,
submarine compared to the urban
bloom of PCH knocking next door.

Drowning in resignation, I was directionless
in my home. I took a wrong turn somewhere.
Husband twice removed, loud love twice lost

because we agreed this time. We must
wait, see. How many hands reach for a page,
or a period, to anchor the enormity

of a twelve-year love story? I gentled my hold
on the steering wheel of my smoke gray hatchback,
focused my gaze on the lights. *This is the only road*

home. Puncturing my panic, a single laugh
lurched through my lips. A song
shocked my body into breath,

into faith. Faith that the kind of love I yearn for
exists, because it lives in me.
I believe in you, too.

The Jewel

It's the first warm day of the season
and our doubts ran off to sunbathe.
At low tide, little hand mirrors
reveal shimmering pools of life,
uncanny reflections of our minds
gushing with memories, daydreams.

What is synchronicity if not seesawing
through a decade of serendipity?

Climbing from rock to rock,
we sidestep that recurring, roaring truth:
The longer we stray, the stronger we land.

Time hasn't changed a thing
and it's changed everything. Let's stay;
watch the water erode our excuses
and reveal what was alive
under the surface all along.
Let's leave our insecurities on the shore.

Can you hear it too? The vibrancy
between us buzzes like bees. Sweetness swells;
pulls me in, leaves me wanting
more. I ache for a life never lived.

Can you see our blooms flickering
in the citrine sun?

Paint me a picture of your mind
so I can see every part of you.
I'll wear that little black dress you like.
It'll be like the first time.
Haven't you learned by now?

Love is stronger than any sound.
Let me show you just how loud we can be.

Claustrophobic Dominos

i.

Slowly, silence turned to
nothing, turned to
something, turned to
demanding to be messy,
because messy is poetic
and messy is sincere
and my dear,
we are only lucky
to be so grand.

ii.

Which part of us is pretending:
the part that believes we don't have a chance
or the part that says we have a choice?

iii.

Remember when
a whisper was too loud
and one word was too much?

iv.

Because one word
was tied to three,
bound to four, plus
a lifetime more.

I told you the truth
when I said:
Once I resume love
I won't be able to
stop.

v.

There's no turning back
after breaking

open. Why would I want to be
stitched back together

after bursting
at the seams?

vi.

For the first time in my life,
my spine was dramatically
unprepared for love.

vii.

Three years later, a psychic tells me
my word of the year is agape.

Bewildered, I wonder how
my heart can open wider,

how my body can handle
any more claustrophobic soul.

XII. The Hanged One

You were never going
to live a "normal" life.

Grieve.
Grieve hard:
your plans,
the wanting in your chest,
all that can't be held
in your hands.

Let your sorrow sing
as you see a higher view:
the horizons
unfurling because you dared
to dream anew

again.

I Wish I Could Convince You

How serious it is,
how it isn't serious at all,
how sacred it is to be silly,
how sacred it is to seriously care,
how little I expect you to care—
until you catch your eyes and laugh
lines in the mirror and your
first instinct is love.

Lion's Breath

Ease isn't an arrival or exclusion.
Ease is a lion's mane, its shape
flickering as fire endures.

Ease burns the radius of your known,
igniting pages of sorry pause and fabricated flow,
illuminating tendrils of new terrain.

In the smoldering, let the melody
soften your ears, neck, chest.

Your heart's heat is somehow still alive,
bellowing your soul's unquestioning.

When You Become

You don't care, as in
shame can't lie here.
Your importance is in you.
Glow unloudly, unbrightly.
Your home was huge in much less.

Relearning Love

Ease is trust.
Ease is trusting trust.

The Lion Didn't Ask to Symbolize Courage

Naked, sun-soaked
in my grief, I knew
my body's perfection.

Beyond my mane, my movements,
my panic—even beyond pleasure:
A no rush, no fuss kaleidoscope
of choice transcended freedom.
The safe of the whole world opened
and I stripped one color away to savor.

I was a gold new to me.

The luster of California sun
doesn't command, simply *is*
attention. When my camera sees
nothing but white, my skin feels
nothing but warmth and everything—
a monochrome home.

Dear lion mane, lion body, desert scene,
honey-drenched:

Courage doesn't have to live in contrast.

Love:
Close your eyes.
Nickname your exhales.
Become comfortably nothing
to their names—
partners for life, for a moment.

As you watch them go, let neutrality
fill your mouth with not-yet-words.

Laugh like you did
when a plane took a scoop of the moon
and marched on like an ant in the sky.

Receiving

Ease is delivering your promises
to silk soil and gritty grace.

Ease is not overwatering.
Ease is knowing when to say,

Help. I need help.
Ease is letting it not be a question.

III:
The Answer in the
Question

When You Need Clarity

Leave. The room, the house,
your state of mind or state lines
to find your playground.
The answer is where you aren't
looking, where you forget to.

When You Forget Yourself

What sense is velvet?
Where does tension unwind
and shell out balmy secrets?
What are you holding
up to your magnetic,
magnifying ears?

Remember waiting and wanting
are arrows with no anchors.

A spiral is sacred geometry.
Let it tousle you. Let it reset
you. Let it lure you back out
into the sun, the dirt, the wild.

Healing's Compost

We reveal only the growth
from the seeds that bore fruit,
black gold a distant memory
as we marvel at our meteors of sustenance.

Juice dripping from our chins, we forget
the fragile sprouts that broke through earth to shrivel,
the roots without eyes, the sacrificial prunings,
the sun-dyed and fallen leaves, winter.

At the first sight of sun, we rush
to plant the next batch of promises
in the stripped soil—humming and smiling
like the darkness never existed at all.

XIII. Death

Intention is permission enough
for intuitive osmosis to begin.

At first, a ripple,
a chirp in your periphery—
wisdom incubating as you dream;

followed by a foggy unforgetting
that feels more like reality
than life;

then, the crash
into your wake
of knowing.

The Rebirth Center

Every room is a waiting room
into revolving doors, trapdoors, freefalls.
Primed to renew,
you're not ready to land.

In the next room,
your Devil and Soul negotiate
the terms of your wonder
and grip of your roots.

The book on the table brays.

Maybe you crack
open the spine and linger in awe
or you riffle through zebras as you listen
for an opportunity to dash out the door.

You're late for an appointment
to try something new:
clothes, shoes, a hobby, a job,
an identity.

SILENT SOUND

Come back anytime!
We're always here.
Subliminal in the background,
you don't hear a thing.

You're already out the door.

Hide and Seek

We bolster the lessons we find
like shiny new toys and play, play, play
so seriously it doesn't feel like fun—
chasing after, the vestigial
premise of the game.

It's like we can't count a thing
until we believe its name.

Of course, what we hoard hits harder
and speaks less, squatting in the house
of grief. The story still pretends—
whole neighborhoods of knowns
fossilized in every rib.

Omniscient Innocence

When change becomes fruit,
worm through tender flesh
to suck on the sweet.

Tousle the learnings
like your favorite curl
to grease the groove of past pain.

Let sustenance seed graceful stories
on your tongue. Megaphone honey
back into the sun.

We Don't Admit

How long *a little bit off*
anchors us to ache.

How we rename defeat *surrender*
and make it sound like a choice.

How we meet biting rage
between healing and held.

If we try, lion words strike like a plush toy.
Meanwhile, truth rumbles silent under skin:

unheard roars, caged ripples.

XIV. Temperance

Ease is a river that blurs every boundary
of your compartmentalized being.

Ease is hearing your body chirp
what it needs, then pouring.

Ease is finding fortune and farce
in the lessons of surrender.

Ease is an open mouth.

When You Are Ready to Change

Healing is dreaming from hell
and eating the tiniest, imperceptible sparks
of your own cremation until you're bored
by the taste of your own death.

Are the Marks We Don't Make the Masterpiece?

What if nothing noticed was accidental?
What if nihilism was simply a zero on an infinite scale?
What if every touchable broken branch,
disco-dancing damselfly, and rain-pasted feather
were creak-in-the-wall reminders
of curiosity slipped under a seat cushion—
every coincidence, validation
of a divine existence and divine timing?

An unraveling of possibility,
greater than every story ever told;
a mouth too wet and pleasing
to recount the details aloud;
a life best lived and deconstructed
for art and connection,
simplified into lessons
but never reduced to anything less
than meaningful
existence?

Meaningful throats and hearts
and stories and shapes
and knowns and unknowns

and possibilities beyond words
and experiences like screams
we try to describe and we die
before we can take a breath
or lift a pen.

Notes on Impermeability

i.

I made a mistake:
believing people want
to be known;
to know (me);
to know knowing
by its diaphragm,
its murmuring sail.

ii.

Sail is both the object and the action,
the resistance and the momentum,
the breath and the breathing.

How much of being human
is the will versus the willing?

Does *will* feel like a noun or a verb?
An abscess or an abyss
in your body? Does it wander?
Does it wager?

In your answer, I might learn
how you travel—too heavy, too light—
with a storied spine I hope you will unbind
and spill someday, somewhere
that can hold you.

iii.

I know my inquiries
are too pointed.

A tender sharpness;
an earnest palm;
the wonder-filled eyes
of it all, unnerving.

It took me too long to learn care
is a confronting thing.

iv.

Why are we here

if not to fill our hands,
our bodies, our heads

with the breeze
of our hearts?

v.

Our hearts all whistle
roughly the same melody:

Open the windows.
Let some light in.

The sound of rain
can soothe you, too.

The water will dry.
It won't ruin anything.

vi.

Tell me what is
real
in your world.

Invite me into the wind's cheeky caress,
face-to-face with a hurricane's stare.

Tell me what you found
believable until the skies
brushed you with grace
and the trees gripped your toes back.

vii.

I'll tell you something you can touch.
The more I die in metaphor,
the more softly I am reborn,
the more fiercely I am alive.

viii.

It isn't all fun, but I think it's more
than seeking something more.

It's quieter than a high;
softer than a low; a rocking
motion in motion, like a sail.

Will becomes an inside-out appetite,

observing the rushing tides,
simply being still, or not—
letting shapes be shapes.

ix.

Our hopscotching human hearts love
to skip over curiosity into escape.
We are eager to forget to remember
we're all alive inside the same memory.

x.

How many times a day do we lose
the answer in the question?

xi.

Tell me why you believe
we are here now—

such fiery, fickle things
in such impermeable bodies.

IV:
Root in this Body

When You Are Tightly Wound

You must scream—of pleasure,
of rage. Let it escape
through your mouth.
Listen with your lungs
as sound tumbles through
your ribs, breaking loose the
constriction around your heart.

Dai Mai Acupuncture Clearing

I'm a still life
work of art,

a pincushion filling
with fresh blood.

Needle after needle
pricks my raw scales.

Restful air gushes,
razing shame's shallows.

I catch my belly's breath
for the first time. I bathe

in my closing wounds.
I memorize nothing

but how and where to breathe.
Through my eyelets, I watch the surgeons

of my spirit hum and dance,
lacing my sternum wide with optical air.

I exhale relief. My fingertips touch
what isn't chest or flesh.

I suck the world in
like an amphibious fish on dry land.

Does my heart need
to be exposed like this?

Salt Cave

i.

Silence isn't a spectrum of noise—
it's the absence of sound.
Perhaps that's why we're shy
with our own thoughts.

On a cave tour,
the guides turned off the lights.
Only for a moment,
they told us.
This is the darkest thing you'll ever see.
I was 10 or 11 then.
I wasn't sure who was more scared—
the adults or the kids
worried what the adults had
to fear
in the absence.

ii.

Grown now, I see clearly
the thunder of my truth
is always louder when I deny

the eyewall is near.
The whooshing sound
from my hometown
—rural, safe, suburban—
that no one else heard
so I stopped mentioning.
A wind that wanted to carry me or carve me,
I'm still not sure which.

All I know is that I open my eyes
in the salty sea and the blackness of the cave
and vocalize my truth—the storm hushing me
to silence as I scream and sing and sing and sing.

I pray to something—
I'm still not sure what,
I don't care who.
She might be me.

I remember feeling quiet in a crowd
as I spoke and spoke and invited and asked.
I remember proving and self-questioning,
different from doubting what I meant.

When I lose my own interest
how can I expect to find common ground?

SILENT SOUND

I notice my toes, my hands, my ribcage;
pluck certainty from the air by its wings,
swarming in the noise
disguised as a fly.

Bee Sting

The hypocrisy is most rules are worth breaking
and there are rules I may never break in this life.

There is only so much bending I can do in this body.
Molding to my will already cost me every lifeline.

My mind combs and collects my spirit
to fit where I need to be: safe, unseen.

What lives in my skin is not the same as my sound.
Torn paper wings brood like secrets in my mouth—

not meant for consumption, but to stomach
and catalog what's on the tip of my tongue.

When *wants* mature into words, even if they're true,
that doesn't mean they wish to root in this body.

My soul is patient, but a noisy collector.
My body aches for rain, something less precious.

The truth is my courage comes from my soul
and there is a limit to its sound in my throat.

The force of it just can't overtake my touchable world.

Sometimes I do wonder:

will I die a bee
who never used my only sting?

Ultraviolet Pool

If we were all honeybees, is there a place

we'd go when we die to re-rack our stings?

A sort of queue, where we'd each receive

the same report: *Fear got the best of you.*

Do you want to try again? Do you want to be

solids or stripes? And with another break,

the whole world would burst into bruised fields;

all tiny suns and magnetic sweet.

Obsidian

The tension you feel
is your sacred melt calling
for your eyes, your ears, your heart
to suck the juice of what is true,
from the vampiric stories
stored in your body,
in your spirit.

Your body of seven
generations; your body of the earth;
of the stars; your body remembers
its impressions, its fear, its shame;
even if the mind pulls away and
forgets how to remember, why
to remember its love.

Dormant and safe
were never the same. I hope
when you erupt, you celebrate
the rise, the light,
the ash.

I hope you collect
your crystals as proof
of the heavy heat you freed,

heavy you no longer need
to carry in your hide.

X. Wheel of Fortune

My solar plexus sits outside of me—
a ring of reaching. I trace its perimeter
in my mind's eye. My longing
is a zen garden: scenic, unhurried.

I close my eyes and my hands become
lion paws, my head heavy, drool dry
with heat and hunt. I'd like to believe
she's a symbol of courage, but

she's tired of me. She's reminding me
seeking isn't strategic. My lasso of dreams,
my halo of hope is too wide—restricting.
Tightening around connection

keeps me shallow in my depth
of being. To be clear, I am not a shark.
People aren't pawns and I'm not a game.
She—the lion-me—

rests high up in the trees,
says you can't be held when you're circling
your core with a pickaxe, cracking
shell after shell of yourself.

Inside the mirror of my meditation,
under its ripple, I see I'm really a stingray;
soft to the touch when contained;
a sign to flee when wild;

sensitive, maneuverable, gray;
related to the shark but with no teeth.
I trust my intuition; my wanes;
the click, click, click of rage—

the only sound stingrays make.
Heart-shaped flying saucer,
flattened disco ball, gritty bottom-feeder,
painted dot and painted line

depending on your view.
I watch worry in my mind's eye,
dark bursts of lightning like shooting stars.
Explosions look sublime under indigo hue.

Not safe to swim becomes peace.
I belong here. I am meant to fly
electric with my weighted wings.
I am not made of bones.

April

You are too stubborn, too masterful at weaving
self-deception to see clearly what you doubt:

You are worthy of the grace of being known.
Identities are arms branching out to hold

your hands. What do you cling to? Who
is ready to soothe your seek? To squeeze

your palm with an offering? A flower, a coin,
a key to the next chapter of your unfolding.

My Acupuncturist Says I'm Widening

I smile. I know exactly what she means.
It's less to do with pounds
and more to do with the scale
of strain that wasn't mine
to carry but to free.

She mimics the body she met:
shoulder blades cupping a spongy heart;
crowded lungs siphoning shallow breath;
cumulatively deflated clavicles,
clutching for replenishing skies.

She unwinds the narrow chamber
my body resembled: blooming driveways
in my ribs, mirroring my core—
now contraction in reverse—
slowly and gently unfurling.

Every needle unthreads knots
that bound me in; stitches me
into presence, into today's wholeness;
invites me into a home with more rooms:
sunny, curtains drawn, good bones.

My voice is fuller and deeper now,

pitch rising from my belly—amplified,
not caged—by phantom fibroids of grief,
space for sound to reverberate through
my unfurnished lives and patient dreams.

My spine is a power line for birds to gather,
chatter, and when they're ready—fly.
I recognize all their songs. Sensing
is less like flashing secrets in blown out rooms
and more like archives of self trust;

the seeds, the harvests, the feasts evident now.
Muscle memory like forgiveness
lights the edges of my world aglow,
filaments sticky with the sap of knowing.
This is what it means to heal the body.

To show up   unhurried   to receive,
decomposing while you live, delighted to finally meet
your debris as it exits your wake—your spirit
slowly revealing its shape,
its terrain, its world.

Like a glacier trusting gravity,
I drink sky and shore with one mouth;
tongue tributaries into lakes and lagoons;
steep metamorphic maps in my core—

stories springing from the melt.

Defying definition,
a glacier is neither solid, nor liquid.
Its crawl is malleable, crystalline,
an atomic cascade of freely flowing flesh.

We, too, change inside the cracking,
seasons escalating our momentum.
We, too, are solid—goddamn—rivers.

We are barreling home
to Earth's perennially open arms.

Sign Me Up for an Improvised Life

An always-figuring-it-out life.
An always-dreaming-and-still-surprised life.
A play-in-the-depths and grace-in-the-expansion life.
An energy-sensitive and discerning life.
A here's-my-soul-and-here's-reality life.
An I-gave-up-on-perfection-long-ago life.
A carry-my-share-but-not-the-world life.
An unlearning-urgency life.
A social-connection-is-wealth life.
A never-too-late-to-say-the-truth life.
A stringing-the-scariest-words-together life.
A story-as-a-snapshot-not-a-cage life.
A sensory life.
A solitude-is-sacred life.
An honor-my-seasons-and-rhythms life.
A presence-is-healing life.
A tune-into-my-intuition life.
A nourish-my-body-more-every-day life.
A curiosity-and-desire-are-seeds-of-courage life.
A trust-myself-as-a-spiritual-practice life.
A grief-and-joy-coexist life.
An express-what's-true-in-my-heart life.
A life of growth through admitting to love.

When You Are Seen

How do I teach you
that you are close when you feel deceived
by simplicity, by honesty?

How do I teach you
how to spot an ease
you haven't met?

How do I teach you
that you are a masterpiece
when I am your mess?

Lion Daughter

Ease is a grief of late arrival.
I point everywhere and nowhere—
It was right here. It was right here.
All along, the answers: holes in my self-
denial. Absence I stomach more easily
when I bristle my way to gray. That space
around wanting, that permanent air pocket necklace,
that suffocating floatation device was a ghastly cocoon
I wormed, sliced, swayed my way out to escape.

This clearance is new, unfamiliar. A warmth
of kin, of skin unwanting—a worn and weathered
patina. A roughness and rigidity of use.

I am leather in a silk store, hogtied by fluttering.
Unmasking sharpens me, simplifies me, reveals
me—black unmixes into every vibrant color,
prismatic palette in plain sight.

The weight of ink shakes loose page after page,
margins of notes negotiating the truth-
thumping thing alive with pale blue breath.
Paramagnetic, meaning weakly, impermanently
magnetic. Meaning I think I'm inviting you near
to paint the perimeter pastel. It's okay if it blends

with the sky. I think I'm inviting myself to blink
the afterimage away. I'm choosing to live
in the glow beyond envy of cold unknown.

Elements untraversed, character unearned,
comparison ends now. Lion daughter, I was born
through fiery grief into the heart of August.

I think I'm inviting you to blanket the burn
with the softness of what could have been
close. There is nothing left for me in this seeking
circle. Instead, ease is here now, welcome
and late—ushering dates ahead and dissolving
dates lost. A fragile finality, maybe.
Is this asking too much
of my self trust?

I don't think I am asking. I know I am
too late. My grief glistens. My ghosts untether,
haunting the gloaming, clamoring
for dawn's horizon.

Acknowledgments

If you're here, thank you for reading my words and holding space for my story.

Thank you to my editor, Tristan Richards. You were so much more than my editor. You helped me meet myself, become a POET, and transform this book into its fullest expression.

Thank you to my teachers. My public school teachers who gave me avenues to express myself. My Enneagram teachers who made the profound system widely accessible. My spiritual mentors who helped me remember my soul.

Thank you to my therapist and acupuncturists, Marya and Rosanne. You eased me into body that can hold me.

Thank you to the early readers of Notes on Disposition—the poems-I-wouldn't-call-poems—and the first readers of my manuscript. You validated my tender heart and made me more courageous. Thank you to my poetry mentors, Tristan Richards, Jess Janz, and Desireé Dallagiacomo. You helped me find my voice. Thank you to the Unfold community. You welcomed me with fierce warmth, exactly as I am.

Thank you to my clients, who saw me before I saw myself. Thank you to my Shadow Play community. You taught me what it feels like to belong.

Thank you to the friends who stay as I ease into new identities and more soul. To my Mom and Dad, Gilly, Charlotte, Sara, Nana, Opa, Oma in spirit, and the rest of my extended family, thank you for always believing in me, making space for lightheartedness, and sharing in my joy. To Kyle's family, thank you for always rooting for me.

Kyle, thank you for finding me in every decade, knowing me beyond words, and loving every version of me. You make every day easier. I love you.

About the Author

Julia Paige Lemke is an intuitive guide, tarot reader, and poet. She was born in Ann Arbor, Michigan and received her undergraduate and graduate degrees from Michigan State University. Julia's writing has been featured by Meraki Press and Reading Rainbow, among others. She currently lives in San Diego, California with her partner and two cats. This is her first book.

You can find Julia's writing, meditations, and community online at www-julia-lemke.com and @julialemke11

www.ingramcontent.com/pod-product-compliance
Lightning Source LLC
Chambersburg PA
CBHW030508130626
46549CB00007B/2883